Unlock the door to understanding, fulfillment, and success with the simple life lessons of

THE GOLD KEY IN THE MAHOGANY BOX

A collection of enlightening tales
that have touched readers
and listeners with their universal power...

- "To be heard again and again. Marvelous from beginning to end."

- "Because they're all about human realities and dreams, almost everyone can relate."

- "Your fables are packed with powerful images. You paint wonderful word pictures. The lines of wisdom are lovely."

- "You are a gifted storyteller. Do you make housecalls?"

- "I was touched by all your fables. I think 'The Mirror Without a Wall' is especially healing for women. I want my mother to know this one—which makes me think these would make great gifts."

- "You exude a powerful warmth and soothing energy. Thank you."

- "In writing for business, there is a great need for stories to be both a mirror and a window—to reflect us, and to expand our vision."

- "As a student of life I really enjoyed the fables. They all have application to life and the choices that we have to make. We are the creators of our own lives."

D0018648

"Ms. Kamin has written an elegant collection of original fables. Utilizing the traditional storytelling idiom, she fills her fables with gentle inspiration."
—Josepha Sherman,
author of *A Sampler of Jewish–American Folklore*

"Your work has proven to possess a rare transformational quality. [The] fables and your readings permit diverse audiences to leave their busy, predictable worlds and enter a new world of possibilities and expanded creative thinking . . . "
—Mariann T. Johnson,
National Arts Management Consultant,
MT Johnson & Associates,
Minneapolis, MN

"It appears that with the '90s we are going to see increased interest and emphasis on values, and your fables are waiting to be discovered and treasured."
—Lois F. Crane,
Librarian,
Wichita Art Museum,
Wichita, KS

"The fables helped our staff focus on meaning and personal insight which directly applies to their role at Weight Watchers. Your fables are a pathway to our most valuable resources . . . ourselves."
—Anne Moen,
Director of Field Operations,
Weight Watchers—Midwest Region

"What is the value of a fable in the corporate culture? Very often we introduce our seminar participants to many new principles, rules, concepts, requirements . . . unfortunately, over time, very little is actually retained. A fable such as 'The Three Peddlers' illustrates how to teach sales transactional skills. For some reason the fable is retained more readily. The simple weaving of a story line can bring definition and clarity to complex issues, while the name of a fable can trigger tremendous recall."
—Gary Lee, Manager,
Corporate Sales Training,
Cargill Corporation

"Your work gets at the 'gut level,' helping us examine our belief systems that ultimately determine our behavior. I believe that this level of awareness is needed if lasting behavioral changes are to occur."
—Charlie W. Prather, Ph.D.,
Manager,
Creativity & Innovation,
E.I. Dupont de Nemours Company,
Wilmington, DE

THE GOLD KEY IN THE MAHOGANY BOX & OTHER FABLES TO LIVE BY

VARA KAMIN

BERKLEY BOOKS, NEW YORK

A Sue Katz & Associates Book.

THE GOLD KEY IN THE MAHOGANY BOX

A Berkley Book / published by arrangement with
the author

PRINTING HISTORY
Berkley trade paperback edition / October 1992

All rights reserved.
Copyright © 1992 by Vara Kamin.
This book may not be reproduced in whole or in part, by
mimeograph or any other means, without permission.
For information address: The Berkley Publishing Group,
200 Madison Avenue, New York, New York 10016.

ISBN: 0-425-13309-5

A BERKLEY BOOK® TM 757,375
Berkley Books are published by The Berkley Publishing Group,
200 Madison Avenue, New York, New York 10016.
The name "BERKLEY" and the "B" logo
are trademarks belonging to Berkley Publishing Corporation.

PRINTED IN THE UNITED STATES OF AMERICA

10 9 8 7 6 5 4 3 2 1

ACKNOWLEDGMENTS

As I BEGAN TO EXPLORE MY FEELINGS IN RE-sponse to the changing world in which we live, the writing of the fables became my anchor. It would take a twelfth fable, perhaps even longer in length than the fables in this collection, to thank all of the people who have assisted me in bringing the fables—and my vision for them—alive.

My agents, Gareth Esersky and Sue Katz, have provided tremendous support. The publication of this collection would not have been possible without their foresight and direction. I am truly grateful to Roger Cooper, Publisher of The Berkley Publishing Group, for his belief in the project. And, to my editor, Hillary Cige, and the staff at Berkley, I extend my appreciation for their time and attention.

From the inception of the fables and throughout the various phases of program development, so much of what has evolved has been with the support, encouragement and guidance of: Freda Rosen, Mel Bucholtz, Mariann Johnson, Joan Poritsky, Sue Meyers, John Roth, John Rosengren, Marjorie Shapiro, Vicki Stuart, Victor Youcha, Carol Lipschultz, Sharon Anderson, Donna McCarthy, John Harper, Marie Savard, Laura Clark, Donna Wallace, Marilyn Habermas-Scher, Anne Goldberg, Randy Rogers, Lori Line, Molly Majerle, Larry Brust, Anne Marie Osborne, Wendy Fink, Nancy Berry, Rosemary Fairchild, Pam Lampert, Pam Borgmann, Carol Gabor, Joy Sommers, Doug Bruce, and all of the program participants who have shared so much of themselves during the various workshops, lectures and seminars these past few years. And for those individuals who have so generously offered their comments for this collection, I extend my sincere thanks as well.

This list of individuals to whom I have expressed my appreciation would not be complete without my acknowledging Susan Grupa, my Administrative Director.

There have been many individuals who believed in me when my dreams to be a writer were still only wishes, and who are very deserving of my gratitude: Candy Provines, Steven Greenberg, Irene Huddleson, Kris Warhol, Susan Walker, Pati Gelfman, Teri

McCormick, Mariana Lippa, BeBe Botoff, Karen Lawson, Susan Perry, Anne Redpath, Evelyn and Lowry Sheely, Joanne Kaplan, Sid Horowitz, Ruth Borofsky, Sharon Nelton, Rona Cherry, Jesse Kornbluth, Jill Krementz, Janet Harrison, Ellen Joy Fields, Rhody Streeter, Bill Purdin, Judy Lerman, Jeni Bryson, Joe Mallard, Wendell Rayburn, Diana Flight, Beth Summers, Kathy Lahey, Joanne Buerklin, Darryl Armstrong, Sue Weller, Jackie Shaffer, Debra Maley, Pat Wolfe, Zenya Griffith, Kris Thwing, Kit Rogers, Joan Davies, and my brothers, David, Robert, Phillip and Daniel, my sister, Betty, and my dear cousin, Jane.

In memory of my parents, I express my gratitude. Although they died before I began to write the fables, they are, in many ways, reflected in these pages.

And, lastly, I want to thank my husband, Robert, for his continued encouragement to write from my heart. Without his support, the fables would still be buried in the pages of my morning journals.

To RLS—

from my heart to yours.

CONTENTS

INTRODUCTION

FROM THE EARLIEST CAVE DRAWINGS OF our primitive ancestors to today's high-tech Hollywood thrillers, or more quiet literary novels, stories have helped to define who we are and where we are going. They enable us to make sense of a world that often seems random and senseless. And stories help us find our special place in that world.

As Joseph Campbell noted in *The Flight of the Wild Gander*, "The most ancient written records in the most primitive tribal circles attest alike to man's hunger for a good story." Storytelling has always been an essential part of the human experience. We tell stories— and listen to them—often finding something beyond entertainment and wonder, sometimes discovering a deeper, philosophical meaning we can relate to the ordinary events of our lives.

The meaning of a particular story, of course, is not

always immediately obvious. Nor should it be. Each person who reads or listens to a story brings to the experience his or her own emotions and understanding. A story's message will appear slightly different to each of us, filtered through the screen of individual hopes, fears, and desires. Good stories, however, use universal symbols and images to relate their messages, enabling all of us to draw at least some collective meaning and inspiration from them. That's why the best stories are passed on from person to person, from generation to generation.

The fable is one of the oldest forms of storytelling. It was a common part of the oral folk literature of primitive peoples, and first appeared in written form on Egyptian papyri around 1500 B.C. The most famous fables are those ascribed to Aesop, a Greek slave, who lived about 600 B.C., and to Jean de La Fontaine, the seventeenth-century French fabulist poet. India also produced a great collection of fables, called the Panchatantra, which appeared during the third century. Bruno Bettelheim, in *The Uses of Enchantments*, describes fables as short, cautionary tales that "tell by means of words, actions, or events— fabulous though these may be what one ought to do."

The fables in this collection share much in common with traditional fairy tales, where the message is often more elusive. Here the reader must interpret each story, glean a personal message, and put it into action.

In writing these fables, I have attempted to address concerns that are both timeless and topical: What is inner beauty? How do we find peace of mind? How do we overcome loss and grief? How do we renew hope and love? These are the questions we struggle with daily.

The responses I have received from people who have read and heard the fables remind me that story-telling can bring people together in an almost magical way. I invite you to enjoy these fables and to share them with others. Stories can help us transcend our differences and unite us both spiritually and emo-tionally. How you personally respond to these fables will depend on you. Whether they become a means for self-reflection, a starting point for change or just a source of pleasure, I hope they serve you well.

—Vara Kamin

INNER
BEAUTY

The Mirror
Without a Wall

ONCE UPON A TIME LONG, LONG AGO there was an old woman who never had a mirror on her wall. With no looking glass to give her praise or turn her away, she never ever wondered who was the fairest of them all.

One day while walking in the woods not far from home, the old woman came upon a rushing brook. As she passed by, the waters stilled just long enough for her to catch a glimpse of her own smile. Startled by the sight of her face in the shallow sea, the old woman, in an attempt to erase her face, splashed about in the water with the tiny ripples. But with each turn her body became bigger and bigger in the moving mirror.

Although the old woman's face was smudged with coal and wrinkles scored her cheeks, until the moment of her reflection there was never a time when anything but beautiful came to her mind: What she had on her skin mattered not. When the old woman was young she learned from her mama who was blind that, though the beauty upon one's face is a gift, the beauty that rests within is the most cherished treasure of all. The old woman knew that even on the days when she put on her Sunday best, her soul was as naked as the day her body was born.

Leaving her image to rest at the water's edge, the old woman quickly discovered that nothing stands still by the stream. As her portrait, made of the shadows of the sea, floated by with the current that moved the water down a steady path, the old woman saw the truth about life resting on the bottom of the sands.

The eyes through which we see are buried in the heart, while one's beauty is forever reflected in the stream that flows through the center of every being.

The End

FORGIVENESS

The Farmer and
the Plow Horse

ONCE UPON A TIME LONG, LONG AGO, there was a farmer who beat his plow horse until the coat of her hindquarters shone. He was a tough task-master who forced the young mare to work each day from dawn to dusk without a moment's rest.

One day after a morning's beating, the horse

pleaded and begged to be left for dead. Knowing death was the only escape from the crack of the whip, she took her very last breath. Realizing this was the end, the farmer dragged the poor plow horse back behind the barn to bury her in a bed of straw beneath the ground.

Since the season of cold winds and snow shed its winter coat, this dead mare was one of many who had lost her life plowing the farmer's fields of plenty. Soon the farmer's fields lost their life. As he stood alone with his empty plow the farmer began to weep, but even his tears weren't enough to nourish the dry cracked soil that lay beneath his feet.

Sadly, the farmer's cries were ignored by all who heard him sob. Some say the man was really beating himself, and not his mares, for the pain he once had when he was as young as an innocent colt. In a moment of regret and remorse the farmer went back to revive his dead horse. But all that was left was an empty bed of straw beneath the barn.

Angered by the sight of the abandoned hole, the farmer yelled out to his wife with passion and fear, "Where is that useless mare?"

Hearing the familiar cries, the farmer's young wife rushed to his side. While tears fell from her cheeks at the sight of the loss, joy poured from her heart.

Secretly, she knew this mare was safe and that at long last all of the plow horses were finally far from the old man's grasp.

For late at night, while the farmer slept, his wife would slip out of bed and tiptoe off to a world where only dreams have sight. But, before leaving the bed, she would stuff the covers with pillows and place the furry cat beside the old man's head. And for the rest of the night—but before the break of the new day— the farmer's wife would spend her sleepless hours far out of view of the old man's eye. With the help of the barnyard pigs, chickens, and dogs, the farmer's wife brought the dead mares to a distant pasture that lay hidden beyond the fields of wheat and corn. In this field, where there were no tracts of land to plow, the dead mares magically came alive while frolicking under the sun-soaked sky.

And just as the wife was about to leave the hidden pasture, she heard the farmer come to her in his dreams. Weary from wandering about his life in pain, he pleaded to be led to a place where he, too, could quietly graze on nature's land. Though his horses took the beating with the whip, he confessed to his wife that he, too, was dying a lonesome death.

Never before had the wife heard these words from her husband's lips nor had she ever wiped a tear from his eye. While the farmer stood in the middle of his dream, water from his tears began to rise. And just as the farmer was about to drown in his own grief, the horses gathered round and licked the tears from his cheeks. Like never before, the farmer learned from the horses he once beat that, to heal the wounds of the heart, forgiveness begins with one kind thought.

While the farmer was still asleep in his dream, his wife came back quietly and slept by his side. And just as the dawning sun slipped under the half-closed shade, the farmer turned over and showered his wife with a smile. He took her in his arms and said with a delighted grin, "You wouldn't believe the dream I just had."

The End

PEACE
AND
TRANQUILITY

The Old Man By the Mill

ONCE UPON A TIME LONG, LONG AGO IN A land where worry grew like weeds, there was an old man by a mill who grew green grass and daffodils. His secret wasn't in the seeds or the daily sprinkles of water, but in his heart and hands that turned and mulched the soil.

Early one morning, when the day was still dark, a young lad knocked on the old man's window and begged for a talk. Although groggy from sleep, the old man invited the boy in and served his unexpected guest a cup of warm milk.

Just as the sun was waking at dawn, they sat by the window while the old man sang him a song. Without music the old man sang out of tune, but the lad listened and hung on every word while the tale of the old man by the mill began to unfold.

Seven decades ago, the old man told the lad, he was filled with fear and sentenced to a life in prison. But in this jail there were no armed guards that held him behind bars, only his feelings kept him imprisoned.

"When I was young," said the old man, "I raced through life ignoring all the faces that once begged me for a smile. When I was finally caught by the sentries who patrol the sky, my first violation only brought me a citation, but the price of my loneliness far surpassed any threats of a fine. Then, when caught with a head full of worrisome thoughts, I was booked for the crime and sentenced to a life of peace and tranquility. Parole, I was told by the judge and jury, would only be granted if I labored forever with laughter and love. In his closing remarks the judge turned me away to live out my days among the flowers and the trees.

"Although it took several turns of the earth spinning on its side before I learned to appreciate the importance of a smile, as the months faded into the years ahead, the greatest lesson I learned in the long days alone was how to take pleasure in the littlest things. No longer was I in a hurry nor filled with the pressing need to make money; even on the days when my pockets were empty I had more than most rich men who counted every penny. In the days when I strived to have it all, I lost what little I had in my quest to get ahead.

"After ninety marks of my birth I was finally set free to look around the world in which you now live. But before the break of the first dawn I found that my ways without worry didn't fit in. After a day of wandering about, I found the path that led me back to serenity.

"So you see," the old man said to the lad, "what was once the place that served as punishment for a crime I attempted to deny, is now my home forever more."

The End

DISCOVERING

LOST DREAMS

The Dream Man

ONCE UPON A TIME LONG, LONG AGO IN the world past the stars in the sky, there was an old man who was a master at building dreams. To find the man who weaved the dreams, a seeker would have to travel over land and in the sea.

Late one night, just before the Dream Man was

about to fluff up his cloud and put his head to rest on a bed of hope, he heard the ringing of heavenly bells. When he peeked through the slit in the sky, the Dream Man saw a lady of the earth standing off in the mist.

Since the light had not yet turned to day, the Dream Man welcomed his unexpected guest and gave her a cloud of her own for the night. But no sooner had she settled in, the sun began to rise and took the darkness from her eyes. The lady of the earth, weary from travel and the chaos of the world she left behind, had no desire to get up at the crack of dawn. So when she asked if there were such a thing as breakfast in bed, the Dream Man, like a magician on a stage, pulled a bowl of berries and a basket of muffins from his sleeve. But after their feast there were no more tricks, for the Dream Man knew there was work to be done.

Blinded by disappointment and fear in the land where peace and harmony no longer reigned, the lady of the earth lost the hope that once filled her dreams. The dreams that she dreamed were locked inside, barred from being shared with the people of the world. And now, with the task of bringing to the lady's heart what she longed for in her mind, the

Dream Man shared the secrets of how dreams are really made.

To find a place where hope can grow on the sphere that spins below, the Dream Man told the lady that she would have to lighten her load. "It's not the weight that's measured in pounds on a tiny scale," he said, "but the thoughts of the mind that weigh the most."

From the life he once lived, the Dream Man knew the importance of confronting the pain that lingers within. "And once the rubble has been cleared," the Dream Man said, with compassion in his voice and love on his lips, "whoever does the digging will get closer to his dreams."

The Dream Man explained that for some, the power behind a dream is like a locomotive pushed by steam; for others, dreams are seedlings of great trees. But whether you are a train going down a track or a leaf on a branch, the Dream Man reminded the lady that dreams are deeply rooted in the ground of desire. And if you wrap your dreams in hope and hold your thoughts in your heart, your dreams will eventually be all that you, the dreamer, dreams.

The End

COURAGE

The Squirrel
Who Could Fly

ONCE UPON A TIME LONG, LONG AGO, there lived a squirrel whose daily chore of storing chestnuts had become a loathsome bore. Although he had put away more than most squirrels for the winter months, he wanted something other than a treasure trove of nuts.

The squirrel dreamed of flying to a world beyond the branches, bushes, and trees, but never dared to seek out his dream. Deaf to the sound of hope, the squirrel never heard the words of faith in his ears, he heard only the ringing of fear. Lost within the confines of his mind, the squirrel couldn't push past the wall of worry that barred the way to where his dreams to fly lay hidden.

One day the squirrel sat on the fence and counted all the birds flying by. Inspired by their freedom, the squirrel raced up the side of the tallest elm and waited till the light of day no longer shined. All through the night, behind the shadow of the moon, the squirrel dreamed of flying through the air. But the next morning, just as he was ready to take a leap toward his dream, he was unable to soar through anything but the sky of his mind. Although the squirrel's urge to fly continued to well up inside, the best he could do was to race around on the branches below.

Time passed through several cycles of seasons. It wasn't until a cold December morning when the sun's radiant beams filtered through the snow-covered trees that the squirrel felt its warmth magically melt away the worries that once caused him pain.

With a feeling of hope in his heart, the squirrel scurried up the trunk of the tallest elm and waited patiently for the wind to blow. But just when the squirrel was ready to take off on the trail of the first breeze that blew by, the limb that held him high above the ground snapped and left him dangling by his tail. Stuck between two twisted twigs, the squirrel struggled to set himself free. With the world upside down, he no longer saw puffs of white clouds, nor did he see the rays of the sun. The sky became the ground while all around him kept spinning around.

The squirrel, hanging by the limb, remained caught in the darkness of his dream. When he called for a helping hand, none of the other squirrels would come near. Fearing they would lose what little they had, none of them would risk trying to save the squirrel who dared to dream.

The squirrel clung to his life by a limb and waited for his life to end. Yet the squirrel knew that if he did little else with what time he had left, at the very least he died trying to live.

Just as he thought he heard the sound of a snapping limb, a red-winged blackbird swooped down, picked him up by his tail and soared off into the sky. As they sailed past the tops of trees, the squirrel got closer than ever to his dream. Never before had he had so much fun as he did flying through the air with his newfound friend. But no sooner had the squirrel reached for the clouds, than the blackbird brought him safely to the ground.

Thus the squirrel quickly learned that desire wasn't enough to give him wings; if he wanted to fly he would have to learn how to play with the force of the wind.

As he raced about, telling of his adventures and his perilous attempt to sail through the air, none of the other squirrels cared to listen. Soon the squirrel found himself alone. Hoping to be spared the pain of being forever ignored, the squirrel offered those around him all that he had, but even his kindness was turned away.

The squirrel climbed back up the trunk of the tree and looked up at the sky thinking of his deep desire to fly. As the squirrel sat there on the branch just above the broken limb, the blackbird who saved his life swooped down once again and came to rest upon his head. Knowing of the squirrel's longing to live with the wind, the red-winged blackbird told the squirrel that he could teach him how to fly without wings, and if he did it just right, never again would the squirrel have to worry about collecting nuts and berries for the winter months.

To begin the lesson, the blackbird showed the squirrel how to flap his tail and push off with his two back paws. On his first attempt the squirrel landed belly up. Stunned by the fall, his mind closed down and in an instant all his dreams to fly disappeared. As the squirrel struggled to his feet, he tried to hide his fear from his red-winged friend, but nothing could stop the squirrel's tears from spilling down his cheeks. And while the squirrel drenched the parched soil with the water from his mind, the blackbird knew that the squirrel would either get up and try again or simply let his dreams to fly float away.

Not much time had passed when the squirrel, determined to live out his dream, dried his eyes, shook off the dirt from his tail, and scampered back up the tree to reach for the sky. With each attempt the squirrel stayed in the air a little longer until finally he felt he had the wings of a bird.

And when the squirrel looked around to thank his friend, the red-winged blackbird was nowhere to be seen. After searching for several days and nights through the thick brush and tall trees, the squirrel finally found the blackbird resting in his heart. Though he was without wings, the squirrel knew he could now race with the wind.

The End

THE SEARCH
FOR SELF

The Ancient Man
and the
Giant of Stone

ONCE UPON A TIME LONG, LONG AGO IN A land where trees were free to grow and blades of green grass waved to the sky on clear days, there was an Ancient Man who roamed the earth. Too big to make his home in a cave or in a hut, the Ancient Man slept outside beneath the light of the moon.

No one knew for sure why this Ancient Man was old before his time, nor was it understood why, when he was young, he was so much bigger than everyone around him. As the story is told, the name "Ancient Man" was given to him the day he was born and that his size, at birth, caused quite a stir. And when the Ancient Man's hands grew bigger than his feet, fear was everywhere and nobody wanted him near. So, for most of his life, the Ancient Man wandered around looking for a place vast enough to call his own.

One night, after years of traveling through the jungles of the earth, the Ancient Man came upon what he thought was the trunk of a tree, but what he found instead was a giant on his knees. As he drew closer to the figure who was so still, he realized that its form was different from his. For where the Ancient Man was flat and straight, this giant was shaped with curves, and upon its trunk were two mounds formed like the rising sun.

The Ancient Man, spellbound by what he saw, reached out to pick a leaf from the branch that draped over a limb of the giant with the curves. Before he could feel a moment's pleasure, a thorn appeared and pricked his skin. The Ancient Man fell to the ground while the giant who stood above him turned to stone.

The Ancient Man felt great despair and more alone

than ever before. And when the earth responded to his thoughts, the world trembled and the giant made of stone crumbled. Left with nothing but a broken dream, the Ancient Man gathered the pieces that were once the great giant and placed them gently in the sun to grow. Though the days became dark and the seasons shifted, leaving the land barren and brown, the Ancient Man never stopped tending his garden of stone.

Late one night, just after the tides had changed hands at the edge of the sand, a gust of wind, with the force of fear giving it strength, stole the world the Ancient Man had cultivated with care. What once grew below the ground now reached for the sun, and where the ocean waters once flowed, the desert became the ruling land. And when the Ancient Man awoke and saw that all was gone, he cried tears of grief that flooded the earth.

The Ancient Man, though tired and scared, pushed ahead through the dark hours until dawn. With what was left of the earth, the Ancient Man rebuilt his life. In his mind a forest grew. From his memory of taste the Ancient Man created a raspberry bush. But it was the silence that the Ancient Man minded the most. From the sight of a feather that floated by in the air, the Ancient Man recaptured the sound of birds singing in his ear. In this world where the Ancient Man outlived all forms, thoughts became things that flourished long after death.

So in his heart the Ancient Man grew thoughts of the giant made of stone and before his eyes the giant with the curves appeared. And when the Ancient Man watered the ground with laughter and showered the giant with joy, the stone crumbled and the giant inside came alive. No longer was the giant made of stone nor was the Ancient Man alone. At long last, the Ancient Man was filled with love that was buried deep within his soul.

The End

A QUIET
MIND AND
STILL HEART

The Garden in the Maiden's Heart

ONCE UPON A TIME LONG, LONG AGO, there lived a maiden whose job it was to scrub the marble steps in the middle of the town square. And no matter how hard the maiden worked to polish the steps to a pretty shine, her work was never done. For even when she lay down to rest, the maiden scrubbed on endlessly in her mind while desperation and despair chased her from behind. Like the patch of barren ground that surrounded the steps, the soil of the maiden's soul was dry and cracked.

During her days of ceaseless toil, the maiden was a slave to many masters in her mind, while confusion ruled the kingdom that stirred inside. There wasn't a day that passed the maiden by that she didn't hide her dreams in her heart and swallow the tears that she longed to cry. When she spoke to those who wished her a good day, the maiden served her curt words upon a plate of anger, while secretly her thoughts were laced with fear.

One day, in a moment of silence, the maiden's mind quieted down. While standing still she was swept away by the currents of her thoughts to a place in her mind where the present concealed the past. It was here at this juncture in the river that flowed through her mind that the maiden's memory floated to the surface of the stormy sea. While gazing at the image reflected in the mirror of her memory, the maiden recalled the times before the magical moment when she learned to speak.

With eyes that could bring the past alive, the maiden remembered the moment after she took her first breath outside the bubble of her mother's womb.

It was then that she quickly discovered what it meant to be alone; for she cried out in the dark, but no one heard the sounds from her heart.

As the years went by, the crying never stopped, and when the pain brought more tears to her eyes, she often felt the sting of a cold hand across her face. By the time the maiden could count to ten and recite the letters of the alphabet, she saw that life had two sides. While most days proceeded without a worry, there were times in the middle of a passing hour that a cloud would cover the sunshine of her smile. And then the day came when the clouds completely covered the sky of her mind; in place of the smile that once graced her face, tears forever fell upon her cheeks. Closed to the world of laughter and joy, the maiden created her own place to live in the darkness of her mind.

Back then, when life was out of control under the roof of a drunken mother, sleep was all that the maiden had. Blanketed under a quilt of somber dreams the long hours of restless slumber shielded her from the sadness and protected her from the madness.

In her youth, the maiden never strayed far from her home, but when the parting of her parents tore apart her life, the maiden, then barely a year past sweet sixteen, fled one night in the heat of a fight.

For years the maiden traveled alone, forever looking for a place to call her own. With one life ahead and the other behind, the maiden existed between two worlds until the day she found her way to the middle of the town square.

As she stood long enough to hear the sound of silence in her mind, the maiden licked the last teardrop from the bucket of sorrow that welled up inside. With her eyes closed, she suddenly felt alive. Instead of the pain that once ripped through her mind, the maiden found flowers growing in the garden of her heart.

The End

KINDNESS

AND

CARING

The Three Peddlers

ONCE UPON A TIME LONG, LONG AGO, there were three peddlers who traveled from town to town selling pots and pans and bolts of satin and lace. One day, after traveling for hours down a long country road, the first peddler finally reached a path that led to a dwelling. But in place of the landowner's manor he had pictured in his mind, the peddler found a tiny thatched-roof cottage surrounded by a red rose garden.

Wanting to sell his wares only to the rich, he drove his wagon past the cottage, even though the lady standing by the window waved and asked him to please come in. Moments after driving by, the peddler noticed from the corner of his eye that the lady's son was running after him. The peddler urged his old mare on from a slow steady walk to a trot, hoping that the horse's gait would be faster than the young lad's steps. The mare was too slow to outrace the boy, however, and soon the lad reached the peddler's side. Before the boy had a chance to speak, the old man scolded him for coming near. Without so much as a smile or one kind word, the peddler drove off in search of a well-to-do lady who might have money to spend on pretty things and fancy lace.

Once the peddler was far out of sight of the lad, he stopped his mare by the side of the road. Weary from travel, tired and scared, the peddler was down to his very last penny. A fortnight had passed since the peddler's last sale, and now, without enough money for his evening meal, he did his best not to fill his belly with despair. The open road was lonely at night and with the next town a long day's ride away, the peddler knew that his only choice before the light of day disappeared was to turn around and follow the dirt road back to the tiny cottage of the lady and the lad.

Surely, he thought, even the poorest of ladies like to look their best. Perhaps, he said to himself, I could sell her a calico print for a Sunday dress.

When he arrived at their door there was no one around to hear him knock. Then, just as the peddler turned to leave, he heard the young lad call out to his mom that the man with the wagon was standing on their front steps.

Ready to make his first sale of the day, the peddler greeted the lady with a smile, but he really wasn't much interested in what she had to say. All he wanted was to feel two smooth coins in the palm of his hand and find a warm bed to rest his weary head before the sun set for the night.

When the lady asked if he'd be willing to barter a bowl of barley for the strength of his arms, the peddler ignored her offer and tried to sell her a skein of pink yarn. Undaunted by the lady's first refusal, the peddler then tried to sell the lady a fancy dress trimmed with lace. But before he had a chance to take it out of the box, the young lad told the man that he had better get off their land.

As the peddler and his old mare moved slowly down the road, the lady shook her head and said to the boy, "It's too bad the peddler never asked, because all I really needed was a new top for my old soup pot."

Just when dusk had turned into nightfall and all the chores were done for the day, the lady and the lad heard another knock at their door. "I've come to offer you candles and kerosene," said the second peddler, who was standing on the steps. "Go away," said the lady. "We have what we need. We get our light from the sun that shines all day and we sleep at night when it's dark. Why don't you come around some other time when you can sell us something we need?"

The next day when the sun threw off the blanket of the night, the lady and the lad set out to plow their small tract of land. Although the morning was filled with many things to do, the lady and the lad always seemed to find the time to laugh. Sometimes they would even dance and sing under the shade of the old oak tree, for it was here, under the leaves that the tree wore for a hat, that they would weave the strands of their thoughts into dreams that paved their life's path.

When the chores were done and the last dream of

the day was spun, the lady and the lad headed for home. Late in the afternoon when they reached their house, they saw a third peddler standing by the well.

"Good day to you, is there anything that you need?" asked the peddler, who wore a warm smile inside the beard that covered his face. Although the lady still needed a top for her soup pot and wished she could afford to buy her son a new pair of shoes, she didn't even bother to ask how much anything cost. She just told the peddler that she didn't need a thing.

The peddler, though disappointed by the lady's answer, asked if they could chat for just a moment while his horse took a drink from her trough. Not long after the peddler, the lady, and the lad began to talk, the peddler learned that the lady's husband had died just after the last full moon found its way to the sky. Left alone to run the farm, the lad without a dad and the lady without a mate were barely able to make ends meet.

When the peddler heard the lady's dream to sell her bean and barley soup to all those who passed by their front door on the way to town, he encouraged her and said, "Surely you must need something to ladle up your dream."

The lad knew just what they needed and pointed

to the pot that sat by the side of the stove just inside the door. It was then that the peddler noticed that the soup pot had no top. Knowing that the lady was short on pennies he said with great joy that he'd be willing to trade a top for her pot for a handful of berries and a bed for the night in her barn. Although not used to kindness from a peddler, the lady graciously accepted his offer.

When they said good night, the peddler told the lady that he would be off before the crack of dawn and perhaps he'd see them the next time he rode through on the way to town.

Although three months of Sundays passed before the third peddler rode by their house again, neither the lady nor the lad had forgotten the man. Greeted like an old friend when he knocked at the door, the lady and the lad quickly invited him in.

They had great news to share, for it was the top to the pot that the peddler gave them months ago that helped turn their lives around. For days on end, the lady explained, the townsfolk came to fill their crocks with the soup that simmered on her stove. The peddler, the lady and the lad all jumped for joy.

When the lady told the peddler that she never failed to mention his name, the peddler gave the lady a long red ribbon to put in her hair. And just when the peddler thought his day was done, the lady said she could now afford to buy what she could once only picture in her dreams—a new soup pot with a matching top and a new pair of shoes for her son.

The End

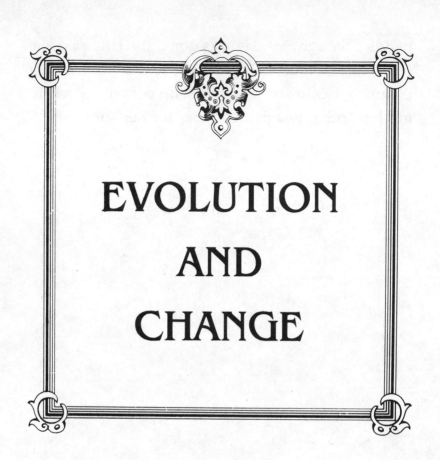

EVOLUTION
AND
CHANGE

The Wings
of the Wind

ONCE UPON A TIME LONG, LONG AGO,
long before the first baby on earth was ever born, the
people of the world lived in the sky. And when the
sky became as crowded as the planet is today, a new
land beneath the sea was formed. It was here, un-

derneath the rushing waters, that a tiny town made of stars was found.

This town, created by the states that were once united and the countries that were once divided, had no ruler. Each person was his own master. Divergent cultures, bound by ancient traditions, stood together while all the land's resources were shared.

When the spoken word was not understood, a smile became the universal sign. The tears of one always touched the heart of another, while joy rained from the clouds. In this town it wasn't silk or satin, but rather kindness and compassion that showed a well-dressed person. And whether one traveled alone or with another on an ox's back, in a carriage or in a cart, it mattered not; it was how people lived their lives that provided comfort, not the chair upon which they sat or the home in which they resided.

Just before the light of the day vanished, all the townspeople put their chores to bed. In this tiny town mankind's labor stayed with the light, while rest and re-creation ruled the night. Pangs of hunger were never felt and no one dined alone. While some folks ate with their fingers and others ate with a spoon, neither the young nor the old ever went without food.

Not long after the evening meal, everyone sat by the firelight that forever burned in the middle of town.

Here, around the brightly colored flames, stories from the old world were told in words that all could hear.

When the world made its home in the sky, many of those who lived upon the orb lost their way in life. Some said it was the city lights, burning long into the night, that stole mankind's sight; others said it was the lack of light from within that blinded the mind and smothered the hearts of all.

As the story is told, mankind never slept. While struggling in the stillness of each night's slumber, the world's people tossed and turned as if shipwrecked at sea. And when they sank to the depths of their own desires, mankind's dreams died a lonesome death.

For centuries, the people of the world constantly prepared for war, but no weapon ever designed could defend against the enemy that lay hidden deep within. Savage beasts of anger, buried by strong wills and passion, preyed upon the pain buried in the hearts of men and women; babies were born without laughter and were filled with sorrow. From one generation to the next these sad souls suffered through life without smiles.

Greed ravaged the meadows and blasted the mountains, while desperation and despair polluted the air. Structures of steel grew taller than the trees, leaving mankind to nibble on the leftover scraps of nature's land.

World peace insidiously disappeared and all that was familiar was gone forever. The sun no longer shone below, but shed its rays behind a dark black haze. The stars, having lost their glimmering cosmic design, slowly slipped from the sky. When the four seasons became one on this planet that spread across the heavens, all but a few burned in the heat of the fire. It soon became known that mankind was the arsonist who set the flames of death upon himself throughout the world.

For those who survived, life soon became less of a struggle. The burns on mankind's body were soothed with a salve of tears from those who perished in the fire. Although small pockets of sorrow still lingered deep within, a newfound freedom returned mankind's power. Since jet propulsion had come to an end, mankind was forced to fly once again upon the wings of the wind.

By the force of nature's persistent commands, mankind's wings carried them far, far away from the crusted vestige of the earth to the place beneath the sea which is now the land. The firelight around which the townsfolk sit was built by the wind that carried the flames to the center of town. And it is this flame that burns on endlessly through the light of day and the dark of night that warms the world, from the beginning before dawn, to the end when the last breath is drawn.

The End

UNLOCKING
INNER
POTENTIAL

The Gold Key
in the
Mahogany Box

ONCE UPON A TIME LONG, LONG AGO there were seven souls who lived in a cave. One soul was from the mountains, another from the sea, three souls grew from the flowers and the trees, and the last two souls came from the stars that shone in the sky. The seven souls had traveled far and wide looking for a buried treasure, but before they could find what they were looking for, they got lost along the way. Through the ages many had perished in pursuit of the buried treasure, yet it was the endless search of all the seekers that kept the earth alive from one civilization to the next.

In search of the buried treasure, each of the seven souls took a separate path. While the soul from the mountains traversed the rocky terrain, the soul from the sea and the three from the flowers and the trees came upon their paths quite unexpectedly. And when the souls from the stars found themselves in a darkened cave, they weren't quite sure how they fell from the sky.

At first, the mouth of the cave couldn't be seen. Surrounded by weeds of envy, anger, and greed, the cave seemed to be at the end of the trail; yet unknown to the seven souls, the cave was the doorway that led to the new world.

Thirsty from travel, the soul from the mountain, who had the head of a donkey and the body of an ox, went in search of a drink to quench his thirst. When the donkey-ox came upon a pool of melted ice, he found the soul from the sea resting quietly. Curling inside itself, the soul from the sea, who had the head of a turtle and the body of a snail, tried to hide from the donkey-ox, but the mountain soul was too smart to let the moving rock out of its sight.

In a far corner of the cave where hope blossomed next to despair, the souls from the flowers and the trees, who were made from the petals of a rose and the twigs of a branch, placed their roots in the dirt to grow. And while the stars from the sky longed to return to the heavens above, they became the sun and the moon that took the darkness from the cave.

When the seven souls crossed the unseen line at the mouth of the cave, they were hardly prepared for the rigors of the search. Challenged by the past, the donkey-ox wanted to be the ruler of the land, while the turtle-snail wanted only to rest by the sand. The rose petals, left without a thorny spine, longed for their prickly edge. And the stars, confined to the cave, wanted only to shine in the sky. Yet, it wasn't until each soul had passed by the shadow of pride did it realize it was not alone; in the darkness all was revealed.

None of the seven souls wanted to admit to the others that they had come in search of the buried treasure. So for days they sat around and talked in nature's tongue about the worlds they had left behind. Finally, after tiring of telling lies, the souls of the rose petals told the others the truth about their lives; once they lost their luster and fell to the ground they wanted only to wither and die. The turtle-snail, touched by the rose petals' truth, shared its feelings of shame about being locked inside a shell. Even the sun and the moon let their thoughts be known. While they stood there arguing about who was the first to claim the sky, they told of their dreams to light up the world. The donkey-ox was the last to speak. At first, he mumbled and then he sighed before daring to admit, how dumb and out of place he always felt because of his size.

Once the seven souls had told all the lies and hidden truths they once had lived by, the floor beneath them opened and revealed a flight of steps. With no questions or even the slightest hesitation, the stars from the sky went ahead to light the way. The others followed and when the turtle-snail took a tumble, the donkey-ox went to his side. And just as the rose petals were about to make their descent, they decided to remain where it was safe. But all the while they tried to hold on tight, the gentle force of nature loosened their roots and pushed them down the flight of steps. Faced with uncertainty, the seven souls moved ahead.

They hadn't traveled far before they came upon a white-winged bird sitting on a carved mahogany box.

But before the seven souls could utter a word, the white-winged bird who had sat before them disappeared in a cloud of smoke. Just as they were about to reach out and unlatch the lid, the white-winged bird reappeared and beckoned them to come near. Without a word, the seven souls obeyed.

It was the turtle-snail who spoke up first and asked the white-winged bird if they could look inside the mahogany box. "Never," said the white-winged bird to the seven souls, "will you ever again have to search for the buried treasure." It was then the white-winged bird told the seven souls to close their eyes and push past the sight of their dreams to a place in their minds where their hearts were still. The donkey-ox had to travel past the purple mountain he had hoped to call his own; the turtle-snail had to crawl out of the sand at the edge of the crystal waters of a protected cove; and the souls from the rose petals were forced to leave the field in which they had forever thrived, while the sun and the moon had to give up the sky. And when they all had journeyed to the place where their minds were clear, the white-winged bird presented each of them with the contents of the mahogany box: a master key, the color of gold, that once had created the world.

As the seven souls, one by one, were given a key

of gold it disappeared within their grasp and unlocked the door to their hearts. "Never again," said the white-winged bird to the seven souls, "will you ever have to search for the buried treasure."

The End

RECONCILIATION

Six Tin Soldiers

ONCE UPON A TIME LONG, LONG AGO, there were six tin soldiers who lived in a land where the trees talked and the flowers whispered secrets between the blades of tall grass. When the trees spoke amongst themselves, they often told tales of the soldiers' cries that once echoed long into the night. Yet it was the sound of the soldiers' tears that touched them the most. And only when the trees were trimmed, or a branch was forced to the ground by a gust of wind, could the bark-bound timber begin to imagine the distress the six tin soldiers once felt.

Forced to fight when they were young in a war with no cause, the six tin soldiers, imprisoned by their thoughts, were never free from the battles they once fought. Although their armor glistened under the moonlit sky and medals of honor were pinned to their souls, the six tin soldiers lived their lives with empty hearts and missing parts.

Unaware of their anger and sorrow, as they grew, they found various ways to numb the pain. One tin soldier locked himself away in a world that never changed. Two of the six tin soldiers endlessly searched for life's secrets while pushing past their feelings that held the wisdom they desperately sought. Another took to the streets always looking for a fight. Late at night this soldier, filled with rage, paced the empty roads sipping a bottle of gin while secretly longing for the taste and comfort of his mother's milk. But it wasn't until one tin soldier began to sculpt his feelings out of clay, and the last of the six sketched his thoughts in stone, did the truth about the senseless war slowly emerge.

Although often laced with lies to protect their minds, each tin soldier had a story to tell. While the thoughts were concealed behind a protective wall, the soldiers struggled with conflicting thoughts. Friends in strife, often enemies at peace, it was difficult for the six tin soldiers to reconcile the past. They each wanted to be heard and have their truths be known, yet when the six tin soldiers stood together they were really alone. When their stories didn't match, they found themselves back in battle as if no time had elapsed.

For years the six tin soldiers created separate worlds in which to live. Strangers even to those who knew them well, the six tin soldiers, with tear-stained hearts, and only a handful of warm thoughts, tried to make sense of their lives. After years of struggle, turmoil and pain, the threads of deception were finally sheared by the truth. No longer covered with lies, the six tin soldiers shed their armor and were able to walk in the world without worry, anger or fear.

The End

For further information regarding workshops and seminars, please send a self-addressed stamped envelope to: Kamin's Fables—P.O. Box 645—Deephaven, MN 55331